Stormy Days

by **Trudi Strain Trueit**

Reading Consultant: Nanci R. Vargus, Ed.D.

Marshall Cavendish
Benchmark
New York

Picture Words

 boots

 clouds

 flowers

 leaves

 lightning

 palm trees

 rainbow

 umbrellas

 window

Look out the on a stormy day.

See  rain.

See flash.

See fall.

See droop.

See  bend.

See flip.

See splash.

See the !

Words to Know

bend
> to fold over

droop
> to hang down

flash
> to make a short burst of light

flip
> to turn over

Find Out More

Books

Herriges, Ann. *Lightning*. Minneapolis, MN: Bellwether Media, 2006.

Paul, Gill. *See-Through Storms*. Philadelphia, PA: Running Press Kids, 2006.

DVD

Storms. Disney Educational Productions, 2005.

Web Sites

National Weather Service: Lightning Safety for Kids
www.lightningsafety.noaa.gov/kids.htm

Web Weather for Kids: Thunderstorms and Tornadoes
http://eo.ucar.edu/webweather/thunderhome.html

About the Author

Trudi Strain Trueit likes a good storm. Living in Seattle she gets to see plenty of them! A former television weather forecaster for KAPP TV in Yakima, Washington, and KREM TV in Spokane, Washington, she wrote her first book for children about clouds. She has written more than forty nonfiction titles for kids covering such topics as rain, snow, hail, tornadoes, and storm chasing. Trudi writes fiction, too, and is the author of the popular *Julep O'Toole* series for middle grade readers. You can read more about Trudi and her books at **www.truditrueit.com**.

About the Reading Consultant

Nanci R. Vargus, Ed.D., used to teach first grade. Now she works at the University of Indianapolis. Nanci helps young people become teachers. She has experienced storms on five of the seven continents— Asia, Australia, Europe, North America, and South America.

Marshall Cavendish Benchmark
99 White Plains Road
Tarrytown, NY 10591-5502
www.marshallcavendish.us

Library of Congress Cataloging-In-Publication Data
Trueit, Trudi Strain.
Stormy days / by Trudi Strain Trueit.
       p. cm. — (Benchmark Rebus. Weather watch)
Includes bibliographical references.
Summary: "Easy to read text with rebuses explores what happens on stormy days"—Provided by publisher.
    ISBN 978-0-7614-4016-1
1. Storms—Juvenile literature. 2. Weather—Juvenile literature. I. Title.
QC941.3.T78 2010
551.55—dc22
       2008030120

Editor: Christine Florie
Publisher: Michelle Bisson
Art Director: Anahid Hamparian
Series Designer: Virginia Pope

Photo research by Connie Gardner

Rebus images, with the exception of lightning and rainbow, provided courtesy of *Dorling Kindersley.*

Cover photo by Polka Dot Images/Jupiter Images

The photographs in this book are used by permission and through the courtesy of:
Photo Researchers: p. 3, Paul G. Adam (rainbow); *SuperStock*: p. 2, Stock Image (lightning); p. 9, age footstock; *Photo Edit*: p. 5, Frank Siteman; *Jupiter Images*: p. 7, Roam Images; *Getty Images*: p. 11, Brendan Tobin; p. 17, Patrick Lin; p. 21, Steve Saburshak; *Digital Railroad*: p. 13, JTB photo; p. 15, Meredith Castlegate; p. 19, Darlene Bordwell.

Printed in Malaysia
1 3 5 6 4 2